Awakening to understand the great value of life and its transcendence.

To go against Nature,

it is going in against the Life,

going against Life,

it is going against God,

going against God,

it is going to die forever.

We'll save the world,

respecting to Nature.

It was necessary to create first all the Universe, to exist life. It is important to comprehend the tremendous effort to create Life. It is important to ask ourselves, to what life was given to us. The reality is that most people think that we were given the life to be the richest of the pantheon. This is a huge mistake, because the only thing that will accompany us will be our noble deeds, not what is changing as is the power, pleasure and money. Having a positive transcendent life, that is, being whole, responsible, kind, cooperating so that we all have Social Welfare, is what will allow us to have Fullness of Being and to Exist forever, in Whom Life gave us. If we are the richest of the pantheon, our life will be lost forever. Let us awaken and seize our time, which will soon be over, and our life will be full forever.

My parent's marriage

In a small village "Lagos de Moreno" State of Jalisco Mexico, was born my father. He was amazed with the locomotive's steam of the railroad crossing near his house.

At his 15 years' age, he decided work on the railroad system instead of going to school. Started working as a boy who feeds the locomotive with charcoal. He always lived in the system and his life was very difficult, but at the same time knows how to handle his love, "The steam´s locomotive"

He is appointed as helper of the Locomotive's, operator, then studies more, and become to be a full operator of the locomotive.

At that time, Mexico was evolving in his bloody Revolution and that boy knows how to handle guns, help his coworkers and continue his studies in a practical way of the railroads.

Then he becomes to know many people working on the railroads, gets a lot of friends and become to work as a Chef's operator of the revolution trains. Knows a beautiful lady, marries her and become a father of a beautiful girl.

The fight in the revolution increases and he is separated from his wife, but he is in charge of his little daughter. As he is working very hard, decides to put her in a convent where the nuns take care of her.

His life is full of battles in the Revolution. Has enormous dangers, but survive. Now He is living alone fighting in the revolution and time goes by.

Soon to become Superintendent of the Railroad's Division and his assistant has a pretty nephew. They become friends and are in love with her. Her age is similar to his daughter's and become married. His new family grows at the end of the Revolution's time. Becomes Under-General Manager of the Mexican Railroads and becomes to be the last general Manager of the Mexican Railroad System. The President of Mexico, General Manuel Avila Camacho was his direct Superior. Then the main Mexican Railroad owed by English people was bought by the Mexican Government and my father was in charge to buy that organization and signed the purchase of that Railroad. In that ceremony, he takes off the English flag and put in its place the Mexican one. At that time, there was a tremendous earthquake in the Mexican State of Oaxaca. The main city of that State was closed and suffering a lot because there was no way to have communication with that city. The engineers informed they will need 21 days to open access to the city. That would be catastrophic for Oaxaca, so my father was by plane to that place and organized all the available forces to open communications sooner. With great effort and with the help of everybody, it was possible to carry food, medicines and help to that city in 3 days instead of 21. Because of these big efforts, the Governor of the State of Oaxaca gave to my father the medal to the Civil Merit, and won the Medal "Man of the Year" 1n 1945. My fathers had 3 children: Alejandro, Francisco and myself.

Doubts of Faith and facts at my school

Retaking our discussion on motivation, I would like to recount an experience I had when I was in school. When I was in fourth grade, I didn't like to study much, and towards the end of the school year my teacher called my mother and told her that I might have to repeat that grade if I didn't apply myself and make a greater effort. My mother talked to my father, and he became angry, but he told her that if I managed to pass to fifth grade, he would be content and would even give me five dollars. (That was a lot of money for a child back then.) So, I really applied myself and studied a lot, and I promised I would grant those five dollars to the Church if I passed. My teachers were Catholic and taught me that if you wanted things to go well you had to be a good boy, study hard and offer sacrifices and give alms to the poor and the Church. (Now I wonder if they weren't teaching me how to be corrupt, or if I made that promise as spiritual blackmails that came to me naturally due to how I had been raised.) Anyway, at the end of that school year, my teacher told me I had passed all my exams and that I could go on to fifth grade. I ran quickly to tell my parents the good news. My father gave me the five dollars he had promised, which I granted to my parish as I had promised. The following year, as I was looking at the list of rooms assigned to each grade, I noticed, much to my chagrin, that I had been placed in fourth grade again. I asked my teacher for an explanation, and he told me that I had passed my final exams, but that my complete average was poor, and the school board had decided it would be best for me to do fourth grade again. My parents were furious, but, of course, I could not give back the five dollars my father had given me. I went through fourth grade again, and finally I graduated from grade school, albeit with poor grades. When I started high school, though, I became really motivated to study hard, and I graduated with honors. Great motivation was born in me and a strong desire to find the Truth. I found in all cultures and religions there is the sentence: "Who with a sincere heart seeks the truth, the Lord will bless"

Ecstasy was a fact I lived at my school

My teachers were religious persons and thought I prayed a lot. I have had a sad time because I saw some fights between my father and mother. She was very pretty and young and my father very important and strong person but jealous. I loved them a lot, so one night before I was going to sleep and pray in a strong way and asked The Lord to accept my life so that my parents were happy. I went to bed convinced I would die that night, but my parents will become to be very happy.

It was a surprise for me the next day I woke up very happy and full of rest. I gave thanks to The Lord because I was alive and I had the hope my parents would be very happy.

Some days afterwards before bedtime I was to pray as usual and I had a very deep concentration in my prayer before going to sleep. Suddenly I felt as I was with "Plenitude of being and existing" and with a huge happiness. Sometime later I woke up and I was not able to understand what have happened to me. But I had the complete feeling I wanted to come back there because that state I really was complete, happy and is impossible for me to explain with words my feeling in that time. To come back there I was sure will help me to give all my life to help people in great need. So, I had the conviction I would need to become a priest and go to help people in Africa.

I started to think about that project, but I knew I had a great difficulty to learn languages, so I did not start to become a priest.

For me it was difficult finishing school. It was not easy for me to concentrate myself. My memory was not strong. It was very difficult for me to arrive to High School because I had poor qualifications.

Maybe it would be of your interest to know an explanation of ecstasy given by experts whom explain as follows: Ecstasy is a subjective experience of total involvement of the subject, with an object of his or her awareness. Because total involvement with an object of our interest is not our ordinary experience since we are ordinarily aware also of other objects, the ecstasy is an example of an altered state of consciousness characterized by diminished awareness of other objects or total lack of the awareness of surroundings and everything around the object. For instance, if one is concentrating on a physical task, then one might cease to be aware of any intellectual thoughts.

At last I was in High School but I was declared invalid!

When High School time arrived, It was obligatory the Military Service. It started with a medical examination and I saw the physician. He made some measurements and told me; "You are invalid" I asked why was that. He told because I was too high 6 feet 4 inches and too thin. So, he asked me to go away to home. Fortunately, I decided because of that inconvenient to study as hard as possible, avoid waste of my time. I decided to dedicate my imagination to solve homework and study's problems and forget about sex's temptations and erotic fantasies. My High School time would be dedicated to improving myself, and obtain the best qualifications in everything. Also, I would continue with my daily prayer time as the first thing to do when I woke up and at bedtime. My religious teachers invited me to join them and have a life as a teacher as they were with their vows of poverty, chastity and obedience. I did not accept but I finished my High School with Honored Mention. I was ready to start my career as a Civil Engineer at University.

How at University time I was got by a Girl's Epilepsy as a presage for my future

I had decided to spend all my time studying hard to be a success in my career. Also, I decided to forget about my sexy hunger and give total dedication to my studies. But I was short of money, so started as a mathematics teacher for High School students. That was some relief for me. Besides A friend of mine whose father had a small factory to recycle wasted oil for motor card, to send the recuperated oil for Taxis. So, I started to visit unions of taxis and I was convincing them to buy the refined oil produced for my friend's father.

At University, I was all the time taking notes and information about all the matters of my career. A friend of mine had a small car and helped me with the daily transportation from my house to the University. Sometime later my father gave me an old Pontiac which was a marvelous treasure for me. When there was going to be an examination, a group of friends were at my house to study there and be prepared for the examination. I remember that on one occasion we were going to have physics' examination in three weeks with a book of 99 pages, but instead of study we played a lot of board games of little football, so that when there was only one week of the examination we had to study almost all the book.

It was at University a very nice and hard time I had. I never will forget once I was invited to a party with my friends and when we arrive at the party there were pretty nice girls. I went to talk with a precious blonde girl and we start dancing. That was wonderful, but suddenly she squeezes me and I was afraid what was going on. Immediately two girls arrive to us and they told me she was suffering from epilepsy. In that moment, I decide I will never marry a girl with Epilepsy.

My life in University was dedicated to study and to sell refined oil to Central's Taxis, and teach mathematics to High School students. I paid my Social Service by teaching the best way to solve physics' problems at University. I did not have a girlfriend, but I was in love with a beautiful one, so you tried to get her attention and I get and paid a small orchestra working in a very nice restaurant named "Villa-Fontana's Magic Violins", and carry them to her house in down to wake her in the best possible way. At the door of her home they played wonderful songs as "Fascination," "La Vie in Rose," "Et Mantenat," "Awake sweet love of my life" and many other wonderful melodies. But nobody heard the romantic show. Beside that why I only was dedicated to study and work. But this episode will appear in my near future again.

My thesis was about the best way to build a building with steel structure using rivets instead of weld. I was the second student of my generation to be entitled as a Civil Engineer. I felt great gratitude to The Lord.

How in my professional Life I won a lot of money and was lost because of my Conscience?

I got the Civil Engineering's degree at UNAM August 6, 1960

My professional work started working as a supervisor of the constructions at "Modelo's Brewery." I was checking the workers in the construction of a storeroom made of concrete's parabolic-hyperbolic shells. I learn a lot in that place.

After a year in that place I started as Consultant Engineer at "San Rafael Paper's Factory" and then in that factory was necessary to build a storeroom to keep fine paper. I suggested a similar construction than the one I mentioned before. I take care of that opportunity and I said I would be responsible for that storeroom with a size of 131 feet front to 131 feet long, only if I were the designer and the constructor. The factory's CEO had plenty of confidence in me. That is why he accepted my proposition. With that Construction y started my own Construction Company with the name EDINSA year 1963. The design and the construction were a successful reality. Again, I gave my gratitude to The Lord for His wonderful help and protection.

With this wonderful background, I started to have more and more projects and my company started to grow rapidly. I do not remember how I meet a wonderful Man with a very nice family, Mr. Jose Antonio Arias. He had a very small factory where He processed the resin taken from the trees into elaborate ones. Mr. Arias had several stores to sell wood, mainly in Michoacán State Mexico. He decided to build a big factory to process a great amount of resin, because He had the concession to exploit about 300,000 hectares of forest, given to Him by General Lásaro Cardenas, former President of Mexico. He had a Spanish Chemical Engineer in charge of that project and decided to give to me the Project as "Key in Hand" that means make reality the Project and give him the Key to start it working. To do that I needed to hire chemical engineers, electricians, and a lot of experts. The project lasted three years and it produces a big quantity of the best Fumaric, Fenolic and Alquidic resins. Also, I was very grateful to The Lord for His Wonderful Help.

I do not remember how I met an intelligent an honest Swiss Engineer, named Ernesto Bettler; fortunately for me, He accepted to work in my Company EDINSA. Soon we started working for different Swiss companies and everything was perfect.

In 1971 I was chosen as representative of the CICM (Association of Mexican Civil Engineers) to the Congress in Paris France named "Sciences and technics at year 2000" sponsored by "CONSEIL NATIONAL DES INGENIEURS ET DES SCIENTIFIQUES DE FRANCE (CNISF)

In 1973, an important Engineering Company from USA: "Rust Engineering Co" was looking to have a partnership with a Mexican one. I was invited to give the Resume of my Company and I was selected as his partner in Mexico. We built together a lot of industrial constructions with great success.

At year 1975 I was the adviser of the (CNIC) Mexican Chamber of Construction's Industry. I founded the first Training Institute for Construction's workers in Latin America.

Then in 1978 I received an invitation from the biggest Engineering Company from Australia named "Crooks, Michell, Peackock Stewart Pyu. Ltd" They wanted to know if I was interested to be associated with them. Of course, I was and I sent my documents to them. The main Engineering firms of Mexico were interested. Some months later I received a document from them informing to me my company was the one selected for that association. Sometime later I received an Invitation to participate in a contest to develop the whole engineering project, design and supervision of a new Grain Handling Plant at the Veracruz harbor in the State of Veracruz México. The Plant would be financed by the World Bank and it will load and unload ships of 50,000 metric tons at a speed of 400 metric tons per hour. We won and developed the whole Plant. This project lasted about 3 years and was inaugurated by México's President Luis Echeverría.

In the year 1983-1984 I studied in IPADE (Instituto Panamericano de Alta Dirección de Empresas)

In Year 1999 I made a whole edition of my book "Awareness the Meaning of Life" (Tomar Conciencia Única Solución para una Mejor Vida) and I sent this edition complete to all the 9 Mexican Governors of Rotary International in México. In year 2000/2001, the worldwide President of Rotary International Mr. Frank Devlin took as his motto for his worldwide Presidency my slogan "Create Conscience and Take Action" in 162 countries and 29,000 clubs.

PEMEX commissioned my company EDIN to make works of National Priority; the most important was shut down a well that was burning millions of cubic meters of gas per day. We did it successfully

In January 1982, I have saved two million dollars. I had destined that savings as my old age insurance. I thought to put that money in an American Institution to be safer. But my Conscience did not permit me that because I felt that was not licit. I gave that money to my brother who had dedicated all his life to the stock market. He was Promotion's Director of the Brokerage House named CBI. Without my authorization, he invested all that money in Mexican treasury funds known as CETES. In February of that year Mexican money was devaluated at half so in a few weeks I lost one million dollars. At that time,

Mexican currency started to be often devaluated. So only fifteen years later Mexican Money was devaluated 400 times. I lost almost everything.

I was looking to build my Home. When I found a nice girl, I did not notice she was epileptic.

I have been successful in my Engineering and to 30 years old. I thought it would be convenient to be married. I was invited to a nice party to celebrate the anniversary of the birth of Rebecca's birth; that was her name. It was a nice party and we started to be friends. It was a nice relationship although I was not sure to be in love with her. I was convinced about her very good education, her nurse's degree and I noticed a very good educated family and very religious with a brother who was consecrated as a Jesuit priest. I was sure not to ask her to be my girl's friend. But after some months of friendship after a nice dinner in a luxurious and great restaurant, I decided to tell her: "If you wish we may become engaged" So it was not a lovely and sweet dedicatory of my love for her. She answered immediately: "Yes"

On one visit, her mother told me Rebecca had three cysts in her brain. Her mother told me that because she did not want me to remember her later she had not told me about that problem. I did not understand the meaning of that. I only thought I was in need to take care a lot of her. Never had I thought about the possibility she had epilepsy. I had forgotten the incident I have had at my University's time.

I thought to myself: "Then what do I do now?"

I was visiting her frequently and to have dinner at nice restaurants from time to time. But in my deepest part of my heart it was the remembrance of the girl to whom I went to wake up at dawn to the marvelous orchestra of the Magic Violins of Villa Fontana. Unfortunately, she did not wake up, but knew about that fact.

Some months later it was a nice surprise for me when I was working at my office, my assistant told me there were a friend of mine who wanted to talk with me. When I saw her I was amassed? It was the sister of the girl to whom I had carried my wake up serenate! Told me she knew her sister will marry me if I wanted to do that! But at that time, I was engaged with the nurse! So, I decided to tell my girl I really did not want to marry her. So, I invited her to a nice restaurant and when I carried her to her house I told her I did not want to be married, I wanted to know more girls. She immediately told me a magic sentence: "Everybody is going to say nobody loves you as much as I do" That was a very powerful sentence and I was not able to insist. I was not able to hurt her, so my engagement went on and never saw the girl I really was in love with. Why I was so stupid? I was because I ought not to hurt a girl at all now and never. I understood in a wrong way the Christian teaching of my teachers.

Then was fixed the wedding party and assisted the girl I really liked the most, so before the ceremony I was talking all the time with her instead than with my fiancée. Then the sisters of my fiancé arrived near me and literally tugged me near to my fiancée.

Then I walked to the altar waiting for my fiancée, and while I was waiting for her, I prayed in a very deep way to the Lord and I said to Him: "Oh My Lord, by means of this wedding I surrender my life to you"

After the wedding, we have made planed out Honey Moon goes to have first night in New York. So, we arrived to the airport and went to that city. After some hours flying, and near by the NY Airport, the Pilot alarmed everybody in the plane. He told us no to be worried because we were going to see on the runway of our plane a white blanket foam. This happened because the Pilot knew the plane was not able to open the undercarriage so that blanket will protect us in landing. He asked to tighten our seat belts and pray. Really, I was not afraid to die, really, I wished die. The landing was perfect. The indicators were wrong and the plane was in perfect conditions. So, we went to our Hotel, The Waldorf Astoria Hotel, where many years ago when my father was the CEO of the Railroads of México, my mother and myself accompanied him to NY, NY to make some negotiations about the Railroads of both nations, because we were in the final part of World War II. The American Government gave to us the Presidential Suite of the Waldorf Astoria Hotel. Now I was not in the Presidential Suite, but in my first night as a married man. I was virgin also. Was that useful or a mistake also?

Now I remember the sentence of Albert Einstein: "I know two infinites; the infinite of the Universe and the infinite of the Human stupidity, but I doubt of the first"

In my marriage, there were some unique and tragic facts.

My first daughter was a nice girl. We were very happy with that wonderful creature.

Sometime later my wife was pregnant again and in due time was born a beautiful boy. Then I feel to be worried because at night he was not able to sleep easily. He was moving his head continuously without resting. He was suffering. So, I carry him with a physician and after some explorations and analysis he told me I soon had epilepsy inherited from his mother. He gave a treatment which one was done in the proper way and my son recovered. In that moment, I remembered when my mother in law had explained me about the three cysts her daughter had on her head. Really, I believe that was a deceit, a dishonest way to hide that situation. My duty now was to take care of my son and I did it. After that we had two more children. I never take in consideration my wife's epilepsy to avoid more children. Now I question myself if that was a correct way to behave. I believe it was correct to have another two children, or not?

Consequences of the epileptic personality in my marriage

Epilepsy is a chronic disorder that may affect how you feel about yourself and your relationship with other people, such as family, friends, or co-workers. It may be especially important to tell your boyfriend about your seizure disorder so there won't be any unexpected surprises. Keep a positive attitude about yourself and epilepsy, and he probably will, too. Please do not hide that.

After the above-mentioned problems, I received at my office an invitation of the biggest Engineering Australia's firm to participate in a contest to select a Mexican firm to be associated with them. Immediately I prepared the Resume of my company and send it with the great hope to be the winner. Some months later I received a visit of some of their engineers to check my office and they came back to Australia. Some months later I received the notification of being selected as a winner. We signed some papers and waited for the development of that fact.

Sometime later I received an invitation of the Mexican government to participate in a worldwide contest to develop the complete Grain Handling Plant to load and unload Ships in 50,000metric tons at a speed of 400 metric tons per hour at the Mexican harbor at Veracruz México. The funding was going to be done by the World Bank. In this international contest, there were in the competition two English firms, two American ones and from México only was qualified my company because it was supported for the Australian Engineering Firm.

We were in need to present our best proposition to develop preliminary sketch, make the complete design of the plant including the proper port foundation designed to receive 50,000 metric ton ships, a storeroom with a capacity to load and unload 25,000 metric tons of grain with conveyor belts.

The project included the preliminary design of the equipment, so that it would be useful for the manufacturers of the mechanical equipment which would handle grain in ships and in the storeroom for half the ship's capacity and the other half would be sent to a railroad yard to load and unload Railroad carriages of 50 metric tons at speed to load or unload each one at speeds of 12 minutes each one.

To fulfill our offer, came to Mexico two engineers from my partner from Australia. Stay some days here to develop the presentation and came back to their Country Australia. With great hope, I went to present our offer, which was studied carefully. One month later I was informed our association had won the contest.

As you may imagine I was working a lot and with great stress. I really didn't have time for my family. We finished the first steps of our contract and presented our information to ask worldwide for the best companies, to make their proposal for the best equipment which one would handle the grain. There were proposals from Japan, Switzerland, England and United States. Then we were in need to study all the proposals and to choose the best. To do that was necessary work together. So, there were two options: One would require two Australian Engineers to come to Mexico and the other one I would need to go to Australia. I was with great stress and not sure what to do. I decided to go myself one month to work in Melbourne Australia to write and explain which one was the best proposal.

I had a ticket from Quanta's Airways from Australia. The route was going very tiring. From Mexico I flew to Acapulco, then the airplane was to have a scale in Tahiti, then to Fiji then to Sidney and finally to Melbourne.

As soon as I arrive in Tahiti I was amassed with so much beauty. I thought I would like to stay there two days and then follow my trip. I asked if it were possible to make some arrangements and it was possible! So, I went to a hotel there and I spent one night. In the morning, I went to a travel office and I took a trip to the Moorea Island flying in a light aircraft. Then I went to a very typical Hotel where the room was made with bamboos and palm tree. The room was supported by wooden pilots above the sea level. The look of the door was only a hook. I rented a small car a Volkswagen and went to know the Island. There were not enough words to describe the great beauty. I was walking by the shore and I saw a ward "Taboo" (means no trespassing) but I went on and suddenly some girls arrive near me very angry, talking in French language. Told me it was very dangerous walk there because I was in danger to cut my feet with the chorales. So, I came back to my small car and came back. At evening I went to have dinner in a very native restaurant. I was amassed. I saw a couple and went to talk with them. Told me they were in quarantine because the ship where they were traveling had an epidemic. I came back to my room and sleep in a very special wandering way. ¡It was amassing my feelings when I understood I was completely alone and nobody knew where I was. I felt myself free! The next day I come back to Tahiti to go to my plane to Fiji. The plane was to leave at night, fall. The airplane took off and only 15 minutes after that, the pilot told us to fasten seat belt because we were going to come back because the plane had a failure. I really was afraid. The landing was ok and the pilot asked us to leave the plane two hours because they were going to make some tests. I went to a near cafeteria looking toward the plane was being tested. Suddenly I saw the airplane into flame! I said to myself I will cancel this flight and will take another the next day. But it was not possible because there was no space in any hotel. So, I came back to the same plane and it took off again. I tried to sleep but it was not possible for me. Then by the window of my seat I saw flames in one motor again. I asked to the stewardess what was going on. Told me one motor is burning, but please do not worry, it will be out and we will continue with the other three motors.

At dawn, we knew we were arriving in Fiji. Another plane was waiting for us to continue to Sydney. That was another long way to arrive to that wonderful city. When I arrived in Sidney, some engineers were waiting for me. I was very tired. They invited me to have a drink and then I took another plane to take me to Melbourne. I almost faint when I arrived there.

At Melbourne's Airport, there were two engineers waiting for me. They were very kind and took me to the Old Melbourne's Hotel where I was going to be while working with them. I took with myself the proposals I had received by the equipment to handle the Grain Handling Plant at Veracruz to handle grain at a speed of 400 metric tons of grain. I received proposals from manufacturers coming from England, United States, Japan, and Switzerland. I carried with myself all of them to be studied there. After a very meticulous analysis, we decided the best equipment was then made in Switzerland by the firm Buhler the CEO was Mr. Charles Thiele. This manufacturer may be found at www.buhlergroup.com

My trip back to Mexico was nice. The same route: Melbourne, Sidney, Fiji Islands, Tahiti, Acapulco then México. I also arrive very, very tired. My wife was waiting for me. I only wanted to go to sleep. I was not very kind to her. I needed to prepare my documents with our suggestions for Mexican Government on the best equipment for the Grain Handling Plant, so I had a lot of work to do.

I had to deal with enormous challenges in my work and my family

How may we help to have a better world for our children?

My life has been a very difficult one. I have had a lot of dangers, rewards, and a lot of suffering. I have two sons and two girls. Somebody has asked me if I had intended to kill myself. The answer is no but I have studied a lot and learned more about myself to diminish suffering and increase welfare.

Here I present a brief synthesis of my life and in a humble way I suggest methodology to increase our responsibility's senses by conviction more than by laws or threaten. This is a humble gift for my brothers and sisters in Mexico and in United States of America.

Is it possible to pack for our last trip? It will arrive soon. Do we have First Class Ticket for that trip? Is it possible to buy or get it with good connections? Let´s remember how ancient civilizations considered this problem and how they evolved.

It will be interesting to know how these civilizations understand the meaning of Life, and which ones are their main contradictions in their sacred books.

We may say Mankind has destroyed a great part of our planet, instead of taking care of it. There is a lot of violence, social injustice and mainly a lot of people are not responsible. Is that failure the result of the inappropriate teaching of the religions?

Please, let's study how each one of the main cultures understands "The Meaning of Life," and the main proved contradictions of the Jewish Bible or Old Testament, of the Bible of Christians or New Testament, and of the Bible of Muslims or Holy Book of Koran (Qur'an)

This brief analysis will help us to find the best way to increase our responsibility's sense. Take care of our planet, so destroyed now, and in some way "have a first-class ticket for our last trip" With these reflections, is sure violence will diminish, and we will be able to help more our families, friends and whole Mankind by conviction, more than by laws or threatens.

Which would be the path of our life if we had born in a different culture that the one we have?

Let's make a synthesis of the evolution of each one of them, next let's study some of the main contradictions we find in each one, and the visualization about the meaning of life each culture has.

The meaning of life constitutes a philosophical question concerning the purpose and significance of human existence or biological life in general. This concept is through a variety of related questions, such as why are we here? And what is the meaning of it all? It has been the subject of much philosophical, scientific, and theological speculation throughout history. There have been many answers to these questions from different cultural and ideological backgrounds.

Consciousness, and happiness, and touches on many other issues, such as symbolic meaning, ontology, value, purpose, ethics, good and evil, free will, conceptions of God, the existence of God, the soul, and the afterlife. The Scientific contribution is describing the empirical facts about the Universe. Science provides some context and sets parameters for conversations on related topics. An alternative, human-centric, and not a cosmic/religious approach is the question "What is the meaning of my life?" The value of the question about the purpose of life may coincide with the achievement of ultimate reality if that is believed by one to exist. Some scholars have a concise response about these ideas. The meaning of Life means to be able to arrive at the plenitude of being and existing where there is no matter, no space, no time, but Plenitude in Whom gave us life.

It is accepted all over the world that sense of fear started to be the origin of all religions.

When a torment was so strong to destroy the houses of the primitive man, He decided to create a god of the winds or thunderstorms, to have his favor. People believed with some gifts given to that God, will help them not suffer so much. The fear of losing crops moved Man to have a goddess of fertility and established some rituals to give her some gifts, so to obtain better crops.

All talk about God staggers under impossible difficulties. Monotheists have all been very positive about language at the same time as they have denied its capacity to express the transcendent reality. The God of Jews, Christians and Muslims is a God who in some way speaks. The Word of God has shaped the history of our culture. We need decide whether the word "God" has any meaning for us today.

One of the reasons why religion seems irrelevant today is that many of us no longer have the sense that we are surrounded by the unseen. Our culture educates us to focus our attention on the physical and material world in front of us. One of its consequences is that we have eliminated the sense of the "spiritual" or the "holy" which pervades the lives of people in more traditional societies at every level and which was once an essential component of our human experience of the world. In the South Sea Islands, they call this mysterious force manna; others experience it as a presence of spirit; sometimes it has been felt like an impersonal power, like a form of radioactivity or electricity. It was believed to reside in the tribal chief, in plants, rocks or animals. The Latin's experienced Numina (spirits) in sacred groves.

I have written my book **_"Awareness the meaning of Life"_** edited in New York, NY by Vantage Press and now in stores.

By Paul Hertre (Vantage Press, NY, NY)

Foundation for the:

Crusade for Awakening the Conscience, the Only One Project against Violence, without Violence, by Conviction, and the best way all of us become to be: "Citizens of Good Will" "Let's Create Conscience, and avoid violence, by Conviction"

You are invited to join this Crusade by stating.

As a Human being you are valuable...

You have great intrinsic wealth....

Your existence offers great opportunities...

Your life at best is short and should be positive profited....

Why are you more valuable than you may imagine?

For you to exist, it was required to make The Universe,

as the factory needed to create your life.

Seek ways to prove this truth to yourself,

Then teach it to your family and friends.

Also, my book: "Be Responsible and Our Final Journey"

- In this tragic era in which we live, we find more than ever, there are many people who talk about values, criticize, and propose solutions.

- The reality is that most people no longer believe in anything and are desperate for the world economic crisis.

President George Bush won the U.S. presidency with a surplus 5 billion dollars and handed the presidency with a deficit of a trillion dollars. The unjust war that Bush promoted left hundreds of thousands of innocent people dead or injured and Asia Minor are in ruins.

- For many researchers, the source of this tragedy is the lack of responsibility that arises by not giving to life the greatest value it has, and its transcendence. Man transcends its life in a positive or negative sense. Until now, Mankind has wasted our Planet and now is an ill Planet; where there is a lot of violence, social injustice, and suffering. Mankind has transcended in a negative way.

- Let's try finding the origin of so much pain, and if possible giving some suggestions, in a humble way.

I have just finished my book **"Sacred Coincidences"** and its translation to Spanish language as "Sagradas Coincidencias" Amazon has published them.

- In this tragic era in which we live, we find more than ever; there are many people who talk about values, criticize, and propose solutions.

- The reality is that most people no longer believe in anything and are desperate for the world economic crisis.

President George Bush won the U.S. presidency with a surplus 5 billion dollars and handed the presidency with a deficit of a trillion dollars. The unjust war that Bush promoted left hundreds of thousands of innocent people dead or injured and Asia Minor are in ruins.

- For many researchers, the source of this tragedy is the lack of responsibility that arises by not giving to life the greatest value it has and its transcendence. Man transcends its life in a positive or negative sense. Until now, Mankind has wasted our Planet and now is an ill Planet; where there is a lot of violence, social injustice, and suffering. Humanity has transcended in a negative way.

- Let's find the origin of pain in the world. And if possible giving some suggestions,

Please find Gift at

www.paulhertre.wixsite.com/Nobel-Peace-Prize

Unite Mankind in Peace with Noble Peace Prize video https://youtu.be/Aykjd0WYJ78

http://shoutout.wix.com/so/aLimwguL

The six mentioned books I may send to you free of charge in digital format if you ask me to do that to my mail tomarconciencia@hotmail.com

www.ingramcontent.com/pod-product-compliance
Lightning Source LLC
Chambersburg PA
CBHW072015280526
45788CB00005B/2059